HOW TO PLAY GUITAR SONGBOOK FOR CHILDREN

THE BEST SONGS FOR CHILDREN

JAMES RICHARDSON

HOW TO PLAY: SONGBOOK FOR CHILDREN

CONGRATULATIONS! YOU HAVE BOUGHT THE BEST GUITAR SONGBOOK FOR YOUR CHILD. IF YOUR CHILD HAS BOOK 1 'HOW TO PLAY GUITAR FOR CHILDREN' THEN THIS NEW SONGBOOK IS A GREAT ADDITION TO HELP YOUR CHILD BUILD THEIR SONG COLLECTION AND EXPAND THEIR REPERTOIRE.

THIS BOOK SHOWS HOW TO PLAY SOME OF THE BEST NURSERY RHYMES AND POPULAR SONGS WITH REALLY EASY CHORD DIAGRAMS AND LYRICS. PRACTICE MAKES PERFECT AND BY PLAYING THESE SONGS ON A DAILY BASIS, YOUR CHILD SHOULD BE ABLE TO ROCK 'N' ROLL WITH FAMILY MEMBERS IN NO TIME.

COMPLETE WITH EASY TO READ CHORD BOXES, LEARNING GUITAR HAS NEVER BEEN EASIER. INCLUDES THESE GREAT NURSERY RHYMES: - THE ALPHABET SONG - BAA BAA BLACK SHEEP - HEAD, SHOULDERS KNEES AND TOES AND MANY MORE!

THIS BOOK NOT ONLY TEACHES YOUR CHILD BUT YOU (THE PARENT) TOO!

WHAT ARE YOU WAITING FOR? GET ROCKIN AND A ROLLING WITH THE FAMILY NOW!

THE ALPHABET SONG

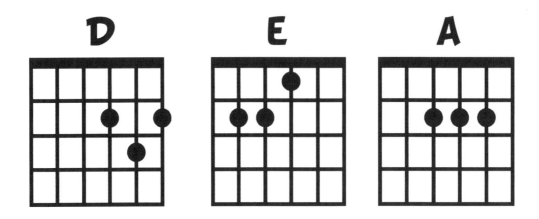

```
A        D    A
A B C D E F G

E   A   E       A
H I J K L M N O P

A   D A   E
Q R S T U V

A D A       E
W X Y AND Z

A             D   A
NOW I KNOW MY A-B-CS.

E         A       E
NEXT TIME WON'T YOU SING WITH

A
ME.
```

BAA BAA BLACK SHEEP

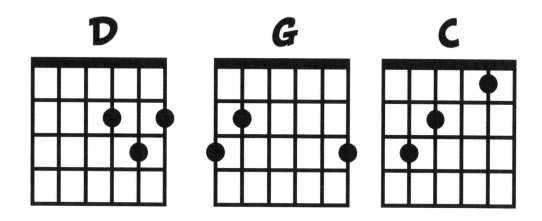

```
G                              C                    G
BAA BAA BLACK SHEEP, HAVE YOU ANY WOOL?

C        G          D          G
YES SIR, YES SIR, THREE BAGS FULL.

G              C        G            D
ONE FOR MY MASTER, ONE FOR MY DAME.

G              C                  G
ONE FOR THE LITTLE BOY WHO LIVES DOWN THE
D
LANE.

G                              C                    G
BAA BAA BLACK SHEEP, HAVE YOU ANY WOOL?

C        G          D          G
YES SIR, YES SIR, THREE BAGS FULL.
```

BiNGO

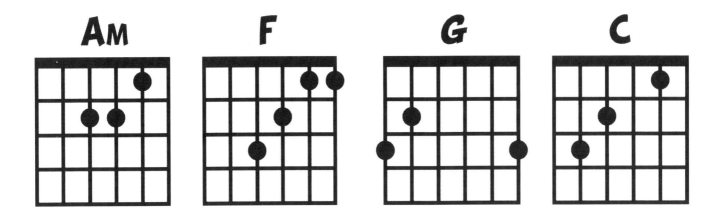

C
THERE WAS A FARMER WHO HAD A DOG AND
                                                             F   C

      G   C
BINGO WAS HIS NAME-O.

C   F
B - I - N - G - O.

G   C
B - I - N - G - O.

AM   F   G   C
B - I - N - G - O AND BINGO WAS HIS NAME-O!

DINGLE DANGLE SCARECROW

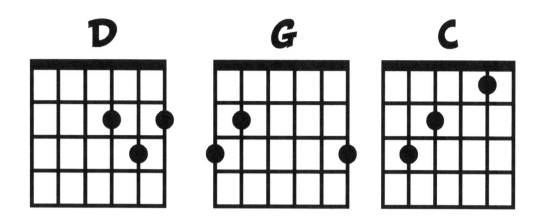

G   **C**
WHEN ALL THE COWS WERE SLEEPING AND THE

G   **D**
SUN HAD GONE TO BED

C   **D**   **G**
UP JUMPED THE SCARECROW AND THIS IS WHAT
    D
HE SAID

        G
"I'M A DINGLE DANGLE SCARECROW WITH A

FLIPPY FLOPPY HAT,

        C   **D**
I CAN SHAKE MY HANDS LIKE THIS AND SHAKE MY
                G
FEET LIKE THAT.

FARMER iN THE DELL

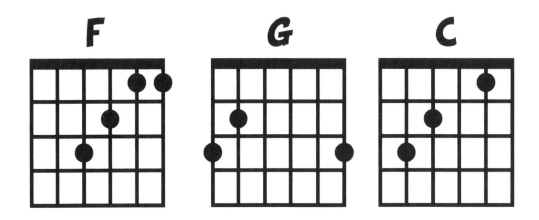

F G C

C
THE FARMER IN THE DELL.

THE FARMER IN THE DELL.

 F   C   G   C
Hi-HO THE DERRY-O THE FARMER IN THE DELL.

2) THE FARMER TAKES A WiFE

3) THE WiFE TAKES A CHiLD

4) THE CHiLD TAKES A NURSE

5) THE NURSE TAKES A DOG

6) THE DOG TAKES A CAT

7) THE CAT TAKES A RAT

8) THE RAT TAKES A CHEESE

9) THE CHEESE STANDS ALONE

5 GREEN & SPECKLED FROGS

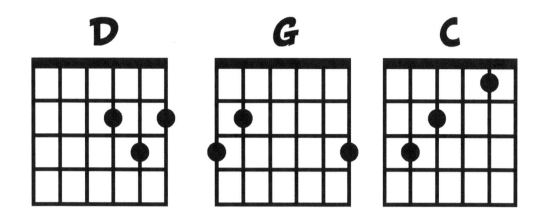

G
FIVE GREEN AND SPECKLED FROGS

C
SITTING ON A SPECKLED LOG

G   D
EATING THE MOST DELICIOUS BUGS YUMYUM

G
ONE JUMPED INTO THE POOL

C
WHERE IT WAS NICE AND COOL

G   D   G
NOW THERE ARE FOUR SPECKLED FROGS GLUBGLUB

FOUR GREEN AND SPECKLED FROGS
THREE GREEN AND SPECKLED FROGS
TWO GREEN AND SPECKLED FROGS
ONE GREEN AND SPECKLED FROG

FIVE LITTLE DUCKS

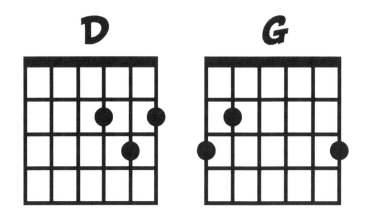

G
FIVE LITTLE DUCKS WENT **D** OUT ONE **G** DAY

D
OVER THE HILLS AND **D** FAR **G** AWAY

G
MAMA DUCK SAID, "QUACK, QUACK, **D** QUACK,

QUACK,"

D   **G**   **D**   **G**
BUT ONLY FOUR LITTLE DUCKS CAME BACK...

FOUR LITTLE DUCKS...

THREE LITTLE DUCKS...

TWO LITTLE DUCKS...

ONE LITTLE DUCK...

FIVE LITTLE MONKEYS

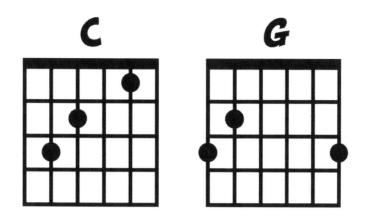

C
FIVE LITTLE MONKEYS JUMPIN' ON THE BED
        G

ONE FELL OFF AND BUMPED HIS HEAD.
                    C

MAMA CALLED THE DOCTOR AND THE DOCTOR
                                G

SAID,

"NO MORE MONKEYS JUMPING ON THE BED!"
        C   G   C

FOUR LITTLE MONKEYS...

THREE LITTLE MONKEYS...

TWO LITTLE MONKEYS...

ONE LITTLE MONKEY...

FRERE JACQUES

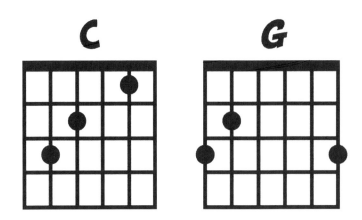

C   G C   G C
FRE-RE JACQUES, FRE-RE JACQUES

C   G   C   G C
DOR-MEZ VOUS? DOR-MEZ VOUS?

C   G C   G C
SONNEZ LES MA-TINES. SONNEZ LES MA-TINES.

C   G   C
DIN, DIN, DON

C   G   C
DIN, DIN, DON.

IF YOU'RE HAPPY AND YOU KNOW IT

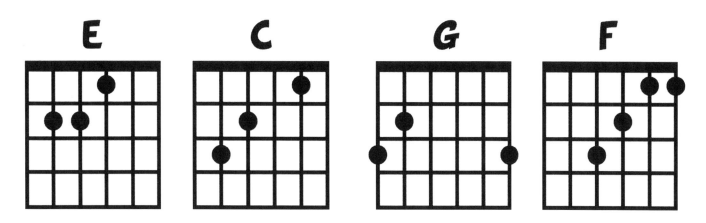

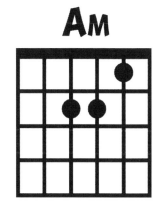

      C
IF YOU'RE HAPPY AND YOU KNOW IT CLAP YOUR
G
HANDS (CLAP CLAP)

IF YOU'RE HAPPY AND YOU KNOW IT CLAP YOUR
C
HANDS (CLAP CLAP)
      F
IF YOU'RE HAPPY AND YOU KNOW IT
         C   **E**   **AM**
THEN YOU'RE FACE WILL SURELY SHOW IT
      F   **G**
IF YOU'RE HAPPY AND YOU KNOW IT CLAP YOUR
C
HANDS (CLAP CLAP)

HEAD, SHOULDERS, KNEES AND TOES

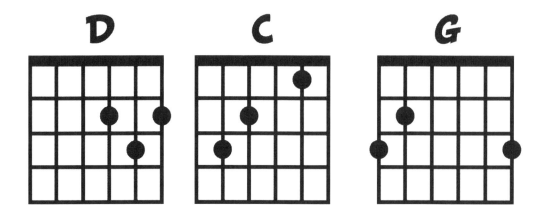

D   C   G

G
HEAD, SHOULDERS, KNEES, AND TOES

KNEES AND TOES.

G   D
HEAD, SHOULDERS, KNEES, AND TOES

KNEES AND TOES AND...

G   C
EYES AND EARS AND A MOUTH AND NOSE.

D   G
HEAD, SHOULDERS KNEES AND TOES.

KNEES AND TOES!

HOKEY POKEY

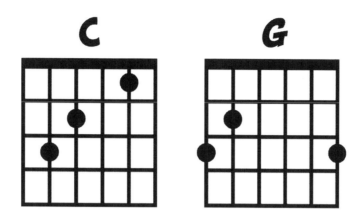

C
YOU PUT YOUR RIGHT FOOT IN.

YOU PUT YOUR RIGHT FOOT OUT.

G
YOU PUT YOUR RIGHT FOOT IN AND YOU SHAKE

IT ALL ABOUT!

YOU DO THE HOKEY POKEY AND YOU TURN YOUR

SELF AROUND.

C
THAT'S WHAT IT'S ALL ABOUT!

HERE WE GO ROUND THE MULBERRY BUSH

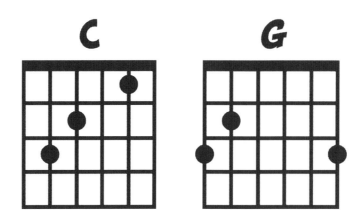

C
HERE WE GO 'ROUND THE MULBERRY BUSH,

G
THE MULBERRY BUSH, THE MULBERRY BUSH.

C
HERE WE GO 'ROUND THE MULBERRY BUSH,

G   C
SO EARLY IN THE MORNING.

HOT CROSS BUNS

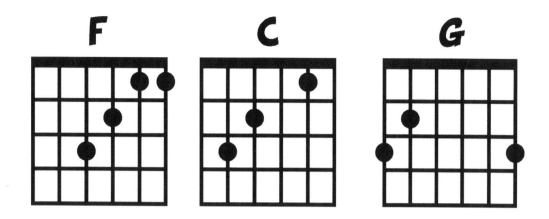

C   G   C
HOT CROSS BUNS.

C   G   C
HOT CROSS BUNS.

C   G
ONE A PENNY, TWO A PENNY,

C   G   C
HOT CROSS BUNS.

C   G
GIVE THEM TO YOUR DAUGHTERS.

C   F
OR GIVE THEM TO YOUR SONS.

C   G
ONE A PENNY, TWO A PENNY,

C   G   C
HOT CROSS BUNS.

I'M A LITTLE TEAPOT

D   **C**   **G**

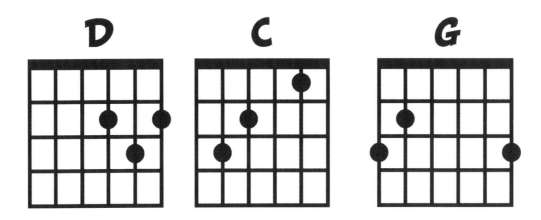

G
I'M A LITTLE TEAPOT

C   **G**
SHORT AND STOUT.

D   **G**
HERE IS MY HANDLE

D   **G**
HERE IS MY SPOUT.

G
WHEN I GET ALL STEAMED UP

C   **G**
HERE ME SHOUT.

C
TIP ME OVER AND

G   **D** **G**
POUR ME OUT.

THE ITSY BITSY SPIDER

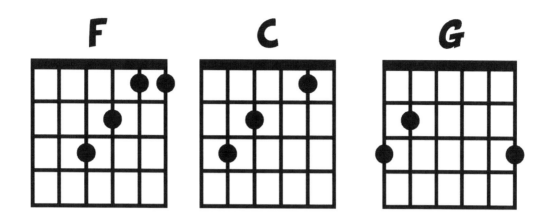

F   C   G

C
THE iTSY-BiTSY SPiDER

G   C
WENT UP THE WATER SPOUT.

C
DOWN CAME THE RAN AND

F   C
WASHED THE SPiDER OUT.

C
OUT CAME THE SUN AND

G   C
DRiED UP ALL THE RAiN

AND THE iTSY-BiTSY SPiDER

G   C
WENT UP THE SPOUT AGAiN.

JACK AND JILL

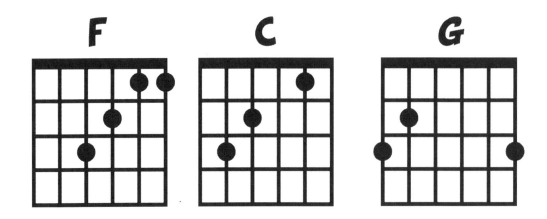

F   C   G

C   F   C   F
JACK AND JILL WENT UP A HILL

C   F C
TO FETCH A PAIL OF WATER.

G   C
JACK FELL DOWN AND BROKE HIS CROWN

F   G   C
AND JILL CAME TUMBLING AFTER.

JINGLE BELLS

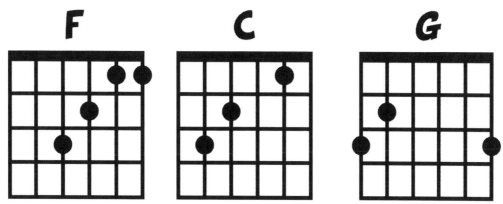

F   C   G

C
JINGLE BELLS, JINGLE BELLS, JINGLE ALL THE WAY.
G   C   G
OH WHAT FUN IT IS TO RIDE IN A ONE HORSE
OPEN SLEIGH, HEY!
C
JINGLE BELLS, JINGLE BELLS, JINGLE ALL THE WAY.
G   C   G
OH WHAT FUN IT IS TO RIDE IN A ONE HORSE
         C
OPEN SLEIGH.
C
DASHING THROUGH THE SNOW, IN A ONE HORSE
OPEN SLEIGH.
G   C
O'ER THE ELDS WE GO, LAUGHING ALL THE WAY.
C
BELLS ON BOBTAIL RING, MAKING SPIRITS
F
BRIGHT.
                 G   F   G
WHAT FUN IT IS TO RIDE AND SING A SLEIGH-ING
         C
SONG TONIGHT!

LONDON BRIDGE IS FALLING DOWN

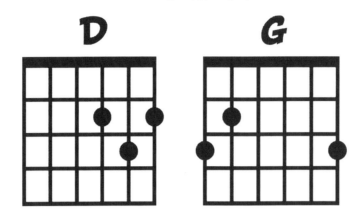

D   G

G
LONDON BRIDGE IS FALLING DOWN
D   G
FALLING DOWN, FALLING DOWN.
G
LONDON BRIDGE IS FALLING DOWN,
D   G
MY FAIR LADY.
G
TAKE THE KEY AND LOCK HER UP,
D   G
LOCK HER UP, LOCK HER UP.
G
TAKE THE KEY AND LOCK HER UP,
D   G
MY FAIR LADY.
G
BUILD IT UP WITH SILVER AND GOLD,
D7   G
SILVER AND GOLD, SILVER AND GOLD.
G
BUILD IT UP WITH SILVER AND GOLD,
D   G
MY FAIR LADY.

MARY HAD A LITTLE LAMB

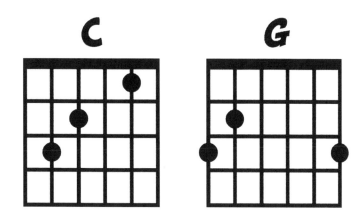

C
MARY HAD A LITTLE LAMB,

G   C
LITTLE LAMB, LITTLE LAMB.

MARY HAD A LITTLE LAMB

G   C
WHOSE EECE WAS WHITE AS SNOW.

AND EVERYWHERE THAT MARY WENT,

G   C
MARY WENT, MARY WENT

EVERYWHERE THAT MARY WENT

G   C
THE LAMB WAS SURE TO GO.

MICHAEL FINNEGAN

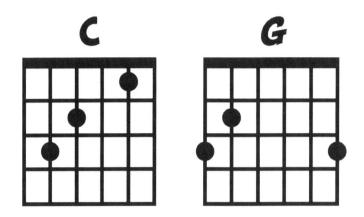

C
THERE WAS AN OLD MAN NAMED MICHAEL

FINNEGAN.

G
HE HAD WHISKERS ON HIS CHINNEGAN.

C
THEY FELL OUT AND THEN GREW IN AGAIN.

G   C
POOR OLD MICHAEL FINNEGAN. BEGIN AGAIN.

OLD MACDONALD HAD A FARM

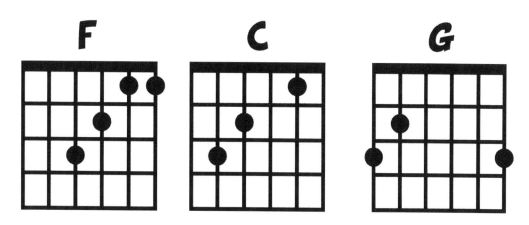

C   F   C
OLD MACDONALD HAD A FARM.
C G C
E-I-E-I-O.

            F   C
AND ON THAT FARM HE HAD A COW.
C G C
E-I-E-I-O.

C
WITH A MOO-MOO HERE

AND A MOO-MOO THERE.

HERE A MOO, THERE A MOO,

EVERYWHERE A MOO-MOO.
C   F   C
OLD MACDONALD HAD A FARM.
C G C
E-I-E-I-O.

RING AROUND THE ROSIES

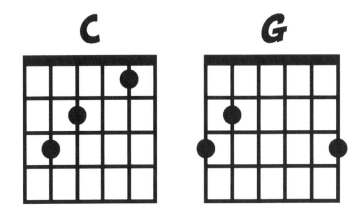

C
RING AROUND THE ROSIES.

POCKET FULL OF POSIES.

A TISSUE, A TISSUE,

G   C
WE ALL FALL DOWN!

ROCK A BYE BABY

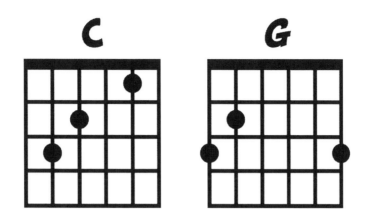

C
ROCK A BYE BABY, ON THE TREE TOP. G

G
WHEN THE WIND BLOWS THE CRADLE WILL ROCK. C

C
WHEN THE BOUGH BREAKS THE CRADLE WILL FALL, G

AND DOWN WILL COME BABY, CRADLE AND ALL.

ROW, ROW, ROW YOUR BOAT

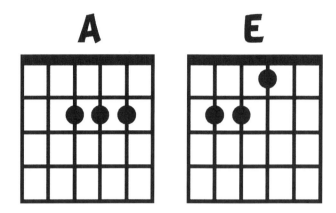

A
ROW, ROW, ROW YOUR BOAT

GENTLY DOWN THE STREAM.

MERRiLY, MERRiLY, MERRiLY, MERRiLY

E   A
LiFE iS BUT A DREAM.

SHE'LL BE COMIN' ROUND THE MOUNTAIN

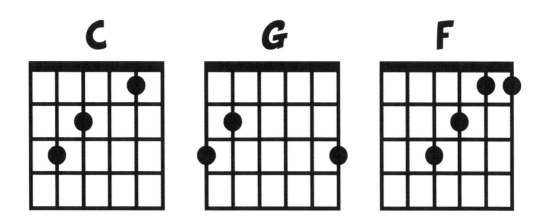

C

SHE'LL BE COMING ROUND THE MOUNTAIN WHEN

SHE COMES (TOOT, TOOT!)

SHE'LL BE COMING ROUND THE MOUNTAIN **G** WHEN

SHE COMES (TOOT, TOOT!)

G   **C**

SHE'LL BE COMING ROUND THE MOUNTAIN,

F   **G**

SHE'LL BE COMING ROUND THE MOUNTAIN,

   C   **G**

SHE'LL BE COMING ROUND THE MOUNTAIN WHEN

      C

SHE COMES (TOOT, TOOT!)

SING A SONG OF SIX PENCE

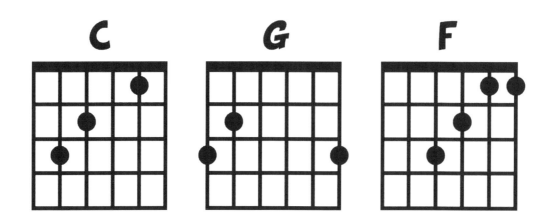

C   G
SING A SONG OF SIX PENCE A POCKET FULL OF

C
RYE.

         F   C
FOUR AND TWENTY BLACK BIRDS BAKED IN A PIE.

           G
WHEN THE PIE WAS OPEN THE BIRDS BEGAN TO

C
SING.

F   G
WASN'T THAT A DAINTY DISH TO SET BEFORE THE

C
KING.

THERE WAS AN OLD LADY WHO SWALLOWED A FLY

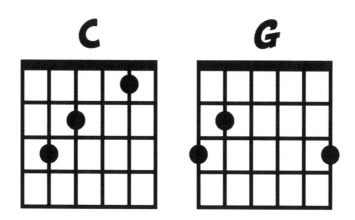

C
THERE WAS AN OLD LADY WHO SWALLOWED A

FLY.
G
I DON'T KNOW WHY SHE SWALLOWED A FLY.
                              C
PERHAPS SHE'LL DIE.
C
THERE WAS AN OLD LADY WHO SWALLOWED A
                    G
SPIDER, THAT WIGGLED AND JIGGLED AND

TICKLED INSIDE HER.
C
SHE SWALLOWED THE SPIDER TO CATCH THE FLY.
G
I DON'T KNOW WHY SHE SWALLOWED A FLY.
                         C
PERHAPS SHE'LL DIE.

THREE BLIND MICE

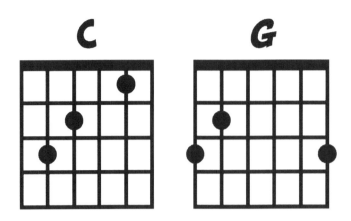

C   G   C
THREE BLIND MICE.

C   G   C
THREE BLIND MICE.

C G   C   G   C
SEE HOW THEY RUN. SEE HOW THEY RUN.

C   G   C
THEY ALL RAN AFTER THE FARMER'S WIFE.

               G   C
SHE CUT OFF THEIR TAILS WITH A CARVING

KNIFE.

              G   C
HAVE YOU EVER SEEN SUCH A SIGHT IN YOUR

LIFE?

G C   G   C
AS THREE BLIND MICE.

TINY TIM

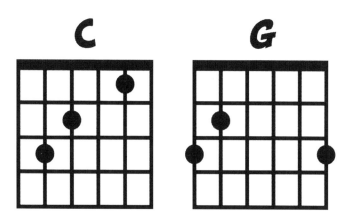

C
I HAD A LITTLE TURTLE,

F
HIS NAME WAS TINY TIM.

G
I PUT HIM IN THE BATHTUB, TO SEE IF HE COULD

C
SWIM.

C
HE DRANK UP ALL THE WATER.

F
HE ATE UP ALL THE SOAP.

G
AND NOW HE'S SICK IN BED WITH BUBBLES IN HIS

C
THROAT.

TWINKLE, TWINKLE, LITTLE STAR

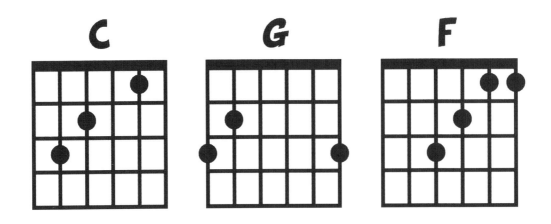

C   F   C
TWINKLE, TWINKLE LITTLE STAR.

G   C   G   C
HOW I WONDER WHAT YOU ARE.

C   F   C   G
UP ABOVE THE WORLD SO HIGH,

C   F   C   G
LIKE A DIAMOND IN THE SKY.

C   F   C
TWINKLE, TWINKLE LITTLE STAR.

G   C   G   C
HOW I WONDER WHAT YOU ARE.

THE WHEELS ON THE BUS

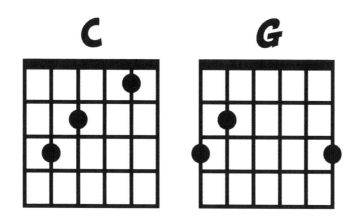

C
THE WHEELS ON THE BUS GO ROUND AND ROUND

G
ROUND AND ROUND

C
ROUND AND ROUND.

C
THE WHEELS ON THE BUS GO ROUND AND ROUND

G   C
ALL DAY LONG.

THE ALPHABET SONG
BAA BAA BLACK SHEEP
BINGO
DINGLE DANGLE SCARECROW
FARMER IN THE DELL
5 GREEN & SPECKLED FROGS
FIVE LITTLE DUCKS
FIVE LITTLE MONKEYS
FRERE JACQUES
IF YOU'RE HAPPY AND YOU KNOW IT
HEAD, SHOULDERS, KNEES AND TOES
HOKEY POKEY
HERE WE GO ROUND THE MULBERRY BUSH
HOT CROSS BUNS
I'M A LITTLE TEAPOT
THE ITSY BITSY SPIDER
JACK AND JILL
JINGLE BELLS
LONDON BRIDGE IS FALLING DOWN
MARY HAD A LITTLE LAMB
MICHAEL FINNEGAN
OLD MACDONALD HAD A FARM
RING AROUND THE ROSIES
ROCK A BYE BABY
ROW, ROW, ROW YOUR BOAT
SHE'LL BE COMING ROUND THE MOUNTAIN
SING A SONG A SIX PENCE
THERE WAS AN OLD LADY WHO SWALLOWED A
FLY
THREE BLIND MICE
TINY TIM
TWINKLE, TWINKLE, LITTLE STAR
THE WHEELS ON THE BUS

13514904R00024

Printed in Great Britain
by Amazon.co.uk, Ltd.,
Marston Gate.